M000194648

REMEMBER THE
Reason

FOCUSING ON CHRIST
AT CHRISTMAS

HONOR HB BOOKS

FROM DAVID C. COOK

REMEMBER THE REASON
Published by Honor Books®, an imprint of
David C. Cook
4050 Lee Vance View
Colorado Springs, CO 80918 U.S.A.

David C. Cook Distribution Canada
55 Woodslee Avenue, Paris, Ontario, Canada N3L 3E5

David C. Cook U.K., Kingsway Communications
Eastbourne, East Sussex BN23 6NT, England

David C. Cook and the graphic circle C logo
are registered trademarks of Cook Communications Ministries.

All rights reserved. Except for brief excerpts for review purposes,
no part of this book may be reproduced or used in any form
without written permission from the publisher.

The Web site addresses recommended throughout this book are offered as
a resource to you. These Web sites are not intended in any way to be or imply
an endorsement on the part of David C. Cook, nor do we vouch for their content.

All Scripture quotations are taken from the *Holy Bible, New International Version®. NIV®*. Copyright
© 1973, 1978, 1984 by International Bible Society. Used by permission of Zondervan. All rights
reserved. Scripture quotations marked NCV are taken from the New Century Version. Copyright ©
1987, 1988, 1991 by Word Publishing, a division of Thomas Nelson, Inc. Used by permission. All rights
reserved; KJV are taken from the King James Version of the Bible. (Public Domain); MSG are taken from
THE MESSAGE. Copyright © by Eugene H. Peterson 1993, 2002. Used by permission of NavPress
Publishing Group; NRSV are taken from the New Revised Standard Version Bible, copyright 1989,
Division of Christian Education of the National Council of the Churches of Christ in the United States
of America. Used by permission. All rights reserved.

ISBN 978-1-56292-882-7

© 2007 Bordon Books

Product developed by Bordon Books, Tulsa, Oklahoma. Manuscript written and compiled by
Rebecca Currington in association with Snapdragon GroupSM Editorial Services.

Cover Design: Koechel Peterson & Associates, Inc.
Cover Photo: © istockphoto

Printed in Canada
First Edition 2007

1 2 3 4 5 6 7 8 9 10

Introduction

SOMETIMES THE CHRISTMAS STORY almost seems like a fairy tale. Its setting within the ancient Jewish culture—so long ago—is far removed from the way we live today. But when we dig deeper, we realize that it is a profound story witnessed by people just like us. Zachariah, Elizabeth, John, Mary, Joseph, the shepherds, the Magi, Simeon, and Anna were real people living in a real place and time. They faced the same fears and questions that we face today. But unlike us, each of them experienced a dramatic, world-changing event—the coming of the Messiah, God's Promise to the world. Through their eyes, you too will witness and be challenged by that cataclysmic event that changed history.

If your heart is calling for more this Advent season, you will be glad you found this simple book. It is specifically designed to help you grasp more fully the significance of the story of the Christ Child. Each day of Advent includes a portion of the Christmas story, a devotional thought, and an opportunity to interact with God through prayer. Inspirational scriptures, poems, stories, and a short reflection on the various names for Jesus are also included. A heartwarming story celebrating God's presence in our lives ends each daily entry. Finally, every seventh day, we've added a special Advent activity you can do alone or with your family.

As you meditate on the truths found in this book, we pray you will experience Christ anew. God bless you on your sacred journey.

THE KING OF
Glory

THE KING OF GLORY sends his Son,
To make his entrance on this earth;
Behold the midnight bright as noon,
And heaven'ly hosts declare his birth!
About the young Redeemer's head,
What wonders, and what glories meet!
An unknown star arose, and led
The eastern sages to his feet.
Simeon and Anna both conspire
The infant Savior to proclaim
Inward they felt the sacred fire,
And bless'd the babe, and own'd his name.
Let pagan hordes blaspheme aloud,
And treat the holy child with scorn;
Our souls adore th' eternal God
Who condescended to be born.

ISAAC WATTS

Simplicity

Let Christmas not become a thing
Merely of merchant's trafficking,
Of tinsel, bell and holly wreath
And surface pleasure, but beneath
The childish glamour, let us find
Nourishment for soul and mind.
Let us follow kinder ways
Through our teeming human maze,
And help the age of peace to come
From a Dreamer's martyrdom.

MADELINE MORSE

The Story of the Christ Child

[READING FROM LUKE 1:1–4 MSG]

So many others have tried their hand at putting together a story of the wonderful harvest of Scripture and history that took place among us, using reports handed down by the original eyewitnesses who served this Word with their very lives. Since I have investigated all the reports in close detail, starting from the story's beginning, I decided to write it all out for you, most honorable Theophilus, so you can know beyond the shadow of a doubt the reliability of what you were taught.

*P*erhaps the hardest thing to remember about Christmas is this: It celebrates the incarnation, not just the nativity. The incarnation is an ongoing process of salvation, while the nativity is the once-for-all-historical event of Bethlehem. We do not really celebrate Christ's *birthday*, remembering something that happened long ago. We celebrate the amazing fact of the incarnation—God entering our world so thoroughly that nothing has been the same since.

As you celebrate Advent this season, make the simple choice to allow God to enter your world—all of it, nothing held back.

Do you see any obstacles in your life that would keep you from opening yourself completely to God?

*The Lord himself will give you a sign: The virgin
will be with child and will give birth to a son,
and will call him Immanuel.*

ISAIAH 7:14

Dear Lord:

Thank You for coming in the flesh to this world. I can't imagine what it must have been like to leave heaven behind and become one of us. That kind of love is too much for my human mind to take in. It's pure, unselfish, perfect. And You have planted that very kind of love in my heart by the Holy Spirit. Help me each day to incorporate that love into my life, receiving it in its fullness and sending it out to others— freely giving to others what I have freely received. You are an awesome God.

Amen.

"Immanuel"

All this took place to fulfill what the Lord had said through the prophet: "The virgin will be with child and will give birth to a son, and they will call him Immanuel"—which means, "God with us."
MATTHEW 1:22-23

GOD WITH US—what a wonderful thought. It is truly the simplicity of the gospel summed up in three little words. Our God was no longer up in heaven looking down on us from on high. He was right here with us, lying in a manger, working with Joseph in the carpenter's shop, eating fish with His disciples, healing the sick, raising the dead. He was God in the flesh, one of us, living here in our midst. What a miracle of grace that was. Jesus now sits at the right hand of God the Father in heaven. But Immanuel is still with us through the power and presence of the Holy Spirit.

The King's Kids

Beautiful, dark-eyed, dark-haired Dana tearfully related her painful experience of becoming pregnant out of wedlock. But her eyes brightened as she explained that while visiting the Crisis Pregnancy Center, a young woman had introduced her to Jesus Christ. Dana received His forgiveness and began a new life. Through hard times as a single mom with a baby girl, she knew that God loved her and would provide for her needs. Dana is now married to a fine Christian man, is actively involved in her church's intercessory prayer ministry, and takes every opportunity to share Christ with others.

The first seventeen verses of the book of Matthew list some of the women in Christ's lineage who had shady backgrounds. There was Rahab, the harlot; and Tamar, who tricked and seduced her father-in-law and had a child by him. Yet another, Bathsheba, had an adulterous relationship with King David. In spite of their failures and sins—and because of God's grace—these women were honored. God redeemed them, allowing them to be remembered as ancestors of Jesus.

The mystery of Christmas is a moment in time when the Incarnate defies human comprehension. Immanuel—God with us, in us, over us, through us. Just as God used all kinds of people to bring His Son into the world, we marvel at how today He works in a supernatural way through ordinary people—sinners—to accomplish His will. God's sovereignty can never be thwarted. ❖

The Story of the Christ Child

[READING FROM LUKE 1:5-7 MSG]

A CHILDLESS COUPLE CONCEIVES

During the rule of Herod, King of Judea, there was a priest assigned service in the regiment of Abijah. His name was Zachariah. His wife was descended from the daughters of Aaron. Her name was Elizabeth. Together they lived honorably before God, careful in keeping to the ways of the commandments and enjoying a clear conscience before God. But they were childless because Elizabeth could never conceive, and now they were quite old.

$\mathcal{G}$od's plan was simple—the pure, sinless life of His Son for the damaged, sin-scarred lives of humanity. Though the prophets had foretold it, the hearts of God's people had grown cold. The son of Zachariah and Elizabeth would serve as a forerunner. His assignment would be to awaken God's people to the news that help was on the way, redemption was near. John the Baptist, as he came to be known, would prepare the way for Jesus the Christ so that His people would receive Him.

Have you received Him? Completely? Unconditionally? John the Baptist was a mortal man and his mission on earth was completed long ago. But today there is another who prepares the way in our hearts—the Holy Spirit. Let Him guide you as you give all to the risen Christ.

How can you prepare your heart to receive more of God?

But when he, the Spirit of truth, comes,
he will guide you into all truth.
JOHN 16:13

Dear Lord:

Prepare my heart to receive You, especially during this sacred Advent season. Teach me by Your Holy Spirit to be the person You intended me to be when first You created me. Thank You for Your plan—a simple, but unspeakably costly plan, a plan that caused You to exchange the pure and holy life of Your Son for my broken and damaged life. Thank you for setting all the pieces in place and bringing hope, joy, and light to my world.

Amen.

"Advocate"

My little children, I am writing these things to you so that you may not sin. But if anyone does sin, we have an advocate with the Father, Jesus Christ the righteous; and he is the atoning sacrifice for our sins, and not for ours only but also for the sins of the whole world.
1 JOHN 2:1–2 NRSV

GOD KNEW THAT OUR HUMAN NATURES would lead us to sin—lead us there and give us a big push. Of course, we are unable to resist in our own strength. Without Him, we go our own way. We continually fall prey to sin. That is the very reason Jesus came, the reason He was born in a stable in Bethlehem. He was born in the flesh, became one of us, lived a life free from sin, died as the perfect sacrifice for our sins, and rose again, conquering sin and death forever. Now, He is qualified to speak to God the Father on our behalf. He is our *advocate*.

The Great Exchange

John Caballero, a forty-two-year-old triathlete and oil-field employee, was working at a petroleum well. Suddenly a pressure-regulating device that had not been properly installed exploded at a force that struck John at up to two thousand pounds per square inch. The blast threw this fifteen-year industry worker thirty feet into a stand of pipes. The result? Brain damage, vision and hearing loss, a broken neck and back, a crushed foot and ankle, a dislocated hip—and he was literally scalped. Doctors said his prime physical condition helped him survive.

Accidents like this are not rare in such a volatile industry, but Caballero's response to the incident is a rare example of selflessness. The company involved was held accountable for the carelessly installed pressure device. A jury compensated Caballero for his medical expenses and lost earnings and awarded a $30 million settlement to discourage future carelessness by any company in the industry. However, Caballero chose to reject the generous award in exchange for a company agreement to implement a safety plan that would protect other employees.

In Craig McDonald's newspaper article, he says, "John Caballero's life has been changed forever. While he is blessed to have his wife of twenty years and two children by his side, he will never work or compete in triathlons again. This ex-serviceman and model employee can never even throw a football with his children. No award, not even $30 million, could compensate him for his losses. But his first concern is still for others."[1]

At Christmas, the Son of God surrendered His throne rights in heaven and became a man, submissive even to His death thirty-three years later. Why? To award humanity with the unlimited riches of His Father's kingdom—and implement a plan that would change and protect their lives forever—all because of love. ✣

The Story of the Christ Child

[READING FROM LUKE 1:8–15 MSG]

It so happened that as Zachariah was carrying out his priestly duties before God, working the shift assigned to his regiment, it came his one turn in life to enter the sanctuary of God and burn incense. The congregation was gathered and praying outside the Temple at the hour of the incense offering. Unannounced, an angel of God appeared just to the right of the altar of incense. Zachariah was paralyzed in fear.

But the angel reassured him, "Don't fear, Zachariah. Your prayer has been heard. Elizabeth, your wife, will bear a son by you. You are to name him John. You're going to leap like a gazelle for joy, and not only you—many will delight in his birth. He'll achieve great stature with God."

$\mathcal{S}$ome people have the idea that in order to hear from God, to receive messages of great import, we have to be quiet, stationary, waiting. It's possible to hear God in such a way. But it is more likely that He will speak to us in simple ways as we go about our daily lives, as we do our jobs and care for our families. Zachariah heard God's message when he was doing his job—the work of the priesthood.

If you are desiring to hear from God this Advent season, listen for Him as you go about your preparations, as you pray for your neighbors and family members, as you reach out to strangers. If you are listening, you can trust God to find just the right moment.

Ask the Lord to remind you of His presence throughout your busy day.

"He who has ears to hear, let him hear."
LUKE 8:8

Dear Lord:

Open my ears to hear Your voice, not only in the quiet of my prayer time, but also in the hustle and bustle of my daily life. I will be listening as I go through my day, just as Zachariah was listening. Because he heard You, You were able to do great things in his life—wonders he could never have imagined. I want that for my life as well. I want to be part of what You are doing, ready and available to do what You ask me to do. Thank You, Lord, for developing in me a listening ear.

Amen.

"Word of Life"

❊

That which was from the beginning, which we have heard, which we have seen with our eyes, which we have looked at and our hands have touched—this we proclaim concerning the Word of life.

1 JOHN 1:1

BEFORE JESUS CAME, only a few heard God's voice: Abraham, Isaac, Jacob, Moses, to name a few. And these heard Him only as He spoke to them with an audible, external voice. But when Jesus came, that changed. Everyone could hear the voice of God, simply by listening to Jesus. He was literally the *Word of Life* to them. Jesus no longer walks on earth, but as believers in Him, we can still hear His voice. He has sent the Holy Spirit to dwell within us and speak His words to our hearts. He has enlivened our spirits and restored our spiritual hearing. If we are listening, we *will* hear Him.

Wartime Christmas Gift

With perspiration dripping from his face, the dejected young soldier trudged through deep sand toward the hooch (a tropical shelter) as memories of Christmases past raced through his mind. There in Cam Ranh Bay, South Vietnam, the Christmas of 1966 would certainly be different. No home-cooked meals, no family celebrations, no fireplace and hot chocolate, and no snuggling with his wife on a cold, wintry night. The officer missed his home. In fact, the emptiness left a crater-sized ache in his stomach and loneliness so severe that he choked back tears.

Then, from a distance, he began to hear the sound of men singing, "Silent Night, Holy Night." Instinctively, he felt drawn toward the melody and followed it to a rustic makeshift chapel. When he stepped inside, he discovered men of all colors and religious persuasions sitting shoulder to shoulder, singing about Jesus' birth. He quietly scooted onto the bench at the back and added his quivering voice to theirs.

In a mysterious way, his emptiness gave way to an inner glow as he participated in the worship service and listened to the small voice within his heart that said, "I have something just for you." The soldier soon recognized and began to appreciate his gift: not one wrapped in colorful paper and ribbons, but a reassuring sense of God's presence and His provision of a spiritual family to offer encouragement and hope.

The Story of the Christ Child

[READING FROM LUKE 1:15–20 MSG]

"He'll drink neither wine nor beer. He'll be filled with the Holy Spirit from the moment he leaves his mother's womb. He will turn many sons and daughters of Israel back to their God. He will herald God's arrival in the style and strength of Elijah, soften the hearts of parents to children, and kindle devout understanding among hardened skeptics—he'll get the people ready for God."

Zachariah said to the angel, "Do you expect me to believe this? I'm an old man and my wife is an old woman."

But the angel said, "I am Gabriel, the sentinel of God, sent especially to bring you this glad news. But because you won't believe me, you'll be unable to say a word until the day of your son's birth. Every word I've spoken to you will come true on time—God's time."

*J*ust like every other person involved in God's plan—the parents of John the Baptist had to take God at His Word. They had to exercise their faith. Zachariah was used to exercising His faith in God on behalf of others, for He was a priest. But this was different. This was about his personal life. Zachariah struggled with his personal faith. God's message to him was unexpected. But with time, he grew in faith and obeyed God's instructions concerning his son.

It's easy enough to have faith in God on a corporate level—standing beside your fellow believers, your church, your family, but what about trusting Him in the daily affairs of your personal life? Is your heart open to hear God's voice to you and you alone?

In what areas of your personal life do you feel God is asking you to follow Him?

Now faith is being sure of what we hope for and certain of what we do not see.

HEBREWS 11:1

Dear Lord:

Zachariah must have thought he was seeing things when there was suddenly an angel in front of him telling him he and his wife—both old—were going to have a child. Like Zachariah, I struggle with my personal faith. When it's just me and You, I start having doubts and second thoughts. What if my mind is just playing tricks on me and what I think You are saying to me is just a figment of my imagination? Give me courage, Lord, to step out in faith and obedience and take hold of You and Your plan with all my heart, soul, and mind.

Amen.

"The True God"

✤

We know also that the Son of God has come and has
given us understanding, so that we may know him
who is true. And we are in him who is true—even in
his Son Jesus Christ. He is the true God and eternal life.

1 JOHN 5:20

THERE SIMPLY AREN'T ANY *unbelievers* in this world—
everyone believes in someone, in something. But believing
alone does not make something true. Stare for awhile at a
piece of black paper. Try projecting all your faith into believing that in spite of the fact that your eyes are seeing black,
the paper is actually white. No matter how hard you believe,
you can't change the truth. We do not simply place our faith
in Jesus because we *want* Him to be the one true God.
Instead, we align ourselves with Him because He *is* the one
true God—whether we believe it or not. Our belief does not
make Him so. He always has been so.

The Power of Faith

Jessie was three years old. Though her father had been out of work for a long time, Jessie's mother smiled and said, "God will take care of us." When her father was offered a job with a small firm located halfway across the country, Jessie's mother smiled and said again, "God will take care of us." And though the move meant leaving relatives and friends behind, Jessie's mother told her with a smile, "God will take care of us."

When Jessie's family finally reached the town where they were going to live, they could not find a place to stay. It was Christmastime, and snow had been falling for days. Travelers were stranded; all of the hotels were full.

Tired and discouraged, Jessie's family turned down a side street and saw a brightly lit sign advertising a special Christmas program that evening at a nearby church. Jessie's mother began to cry, remembering the Christmas program that their relatives and friends back home would be enjoying this year without them. As she wept into her open hands, little Jessie leaned over, gave her mother a gentle kiss, and whispered, "God will take care of us."

Through tearstained eyes, Jessie's mother looked up and gave Jessie a small smile. "You're right, sweetheart," she sniffled. Together the weary young family wandered into the small church and found themselves immediately engulfed in the welcoming warmth of the congregation. Before the program ended that evening, Jessie's family not only had a place to stay, but also a place to celebrate Christmas. Indeed, God did take care of them. ❋

The Story of the Christ Child

[READING FROM LUKE 1:21–25 MSG]

Meanwhile, the congregation waiting for Zachariah was getting restless, wondering what was keeping him so long in the sanctuary. When he came out and couldn't speak, they knew he had seen a vision. He continued speechless and had to use sign language with the people.

When the course of his priestly assignment was completed, he went back home. It wasn't long before his wife, Elizabeth, conceived. She went off by herself for five months, relishing her pregnancy. "So, this is how God acts to remedy my unfortunate condition!" she said.

*H*ave you wondered about God's faithfulness? Can He be trusted? He can. Many people make their own plans and ask God to bless and empower them. When He doesn't do that, they accuse Him of unfaithfulness. But when it comes to God's plan—the truest, most sacred purpose for your life—He is utterly, irrevocably, unconditionally, unrelentingly faithful. If He has said it, He will do it—no matter what! It's that simple.

Zachariah and Elizabeth had been asking for a son for many years. Now she was far beyond the natural age to give birth. But God had a plan all along, a plan to answer their prayers and advance His plan to redeem the human race. Place your desires in His hands. He will not let you down.

Is there some disappointment in your past that keeps you from placing your hopes and desires in God's hands? Are you willing to talk to God about it?

Know therefore that the LORD *thy God, he is God, the faithful God, which keepeth covenant and mercy with them that love him and keep his commandments to a thousand generations.*

DEUTERONOMY 7:9 KJV

Dear Lord:

Each time I make a promise, take on a commitment, allow another person to depend on me, I intend to follow through, to make good. Still, Lord, You know I often fail. But You never fail. You always keep Your promises, make good on Your commitments, and fully support me when I am depending on You—without exception! It's as simple as that. Thank You for Your faithfulness in my life. Thank You for showing me again and again that You will never let me down when I trust in You. Thank You for being the One who is faithful and true.

Amen.

"Faithful and True"

*I saw heaven standing open and there before me was
a white horse, whose rider is called Faithful and True.
With justice he judges and makes war. His eyes are like
blazing fire, and on his head are many crowns.*
REVELATION 19:11–12

THERE ARE NO GUARANTEES in life, no certainties—except
God. Bethlehem's tiny child grew up, accomplished His earthly
mission, and now sits at His Father's right hand. He not only
says He is faithful, He has proven it. No matter what God has
called you to do, no matter what He has spoken to your heart,
you can trust Him to bring it to pass. He won't fail you—can't
fail you. Banish your doubts, step forward, and take the hand of
Jesus. Despite their good intentions, no human being has
earned the designation of faithful and true. Jesus alone can be
trusted completely—He is *faithful and true*.

Shining Lights and Singing Angels

A U.S. Air Force sergeant in Thailand let his light shine. When others were out partying and chasing women, he stayed in, talked to the other soldiers, relaxed, and read.

One day, a young soldier asked him why. The sergeant shared his faith in God with the young man and told him that his relationship with Jesus meant he made different lifestyle choices. The two began reading Scriptures together and praying regularly. The older soldier had the joy of leading the younger man to his Lord.

Christmas was approaching, and the young man celebrated his new birth as the world celebrated Christ's birth.

Due to seniority, the sergeant went home for holiday leave, while some of the others in the unit stayed behind, including the younger soldier. When the sergeant returned, the men in his unit met his plane with unhappy news. The young soldier had been killed in battle the day before.

Though deeply saddened by the passing of his young friend, the sergeant comforted the other soldiers with the truth of good news: "This year, he really did get to go 'home' for Christmas."

A great crowd of witnesses worships at God's throne. In endless praise, those who have gone on to be with our Lord in heaven ahead of us can inspire hope in our hearts. Christmas is a special time to join in the heavenly celebration of joy. ❋

The Story of the Christ Child

[READING FROM LUKE 1:26–28 MSG]

A VIRGIN CONCEIVES

*In the sixth month of Elizabeth's pregnancy, God sent
the angel Gabriel to the Galilean village of Nazareth
to a virgin engaged to be married to a man descended
from David. His name was Joseph, and the virgin's
name, Mary. Upon entering, Gabriel greeted her:*

> *Good morning!*
> *You're beautiful with God's beauty,*
> *Beautiful inside and out!*
> *God be with you.*

*D*o you live in fear that God will ask you to do something you don't want to do—so afraid that you refuse to listen and fail to hear what God really has planned for you? What a tragedy. But you can change all that. God's plan for you—just like God's plan for Mary—is something He has prepared you for all your life. In fact, as you open your ears to hear, you will find that while your assignment might be grander than you imagined, it is consistent with who you are.

God knew Mary inside and out. He had always known her. He had prepared her for her mission since long before she took her first breath. Don't be afraid of God's plan for you. Ask for it. Embrace it. It will be a perfect fit.

Have you asked God to show you the purpose for which you were created? If not, what fears are standing in your way?

There is no fear in love. But perfect love drives out fear,
because fear has to do with punishment. The one who
fears is not made perfect in love.

I JOHN 4:18

Dear Lord:

Banish fear from my life and reveal to my heart what You have for me. I know I am now ready to embrace that truth, believing that You won't ask me to do anything that is inconsistent with the person You created me to be. I know that when Your plan is revealed, it will fit me perfectly. Your Holy Spirit will tell me exactly what I need to know to take each step along the path. Thank you, Lord, for placing Your confidence in me, just as You placed Your confidence in Mary. Help me to follow Your simple instructions that I might achieve great things for Your kingdom.

Amen.

"The Good Shepherd"

[Jesus said], *"I am the good shepherd. I know my own and my own know me, just as the Father knows me and I know the Father. And I lay down my life for the sheep."*
JOHN 10:14-15 NRSV

SHEEP HAVE A TENDENCY to wander. That's why they need a shepherd. In this way, we are like sheep. Without a strong guiding hand, we tend to drift, making unfortunate choices without considering the consequences. Like sheep, we often find ourselves out on a ledge, tangled in brambles, and lost. God knew that we would need a shepherd to keep us on the path of righteousness. So He sent Jesus, the *Good Shepherd*, first to lay down His life for us and then to lead us, ever so slowly and patiently, along the road to eternal life. He knows each of us—our strengths, our weaknesses, our personal struggles with sin—and we know Him because we are the sheep of His pasture.

Someone Who Understands

One Christmas Eve, a man refused to attend church with his wife. He was a good man but could not believe the Christmas story of God coming to earth as a man. So he stayed at home and waited for his family to return later.

Shortly after, snow began to fall heavily. A loud thud against his front door startled the man. When the sounds continued, he opened the front door to investigate. There he saw a flock of birds, huddled in the snow. In a desperate search for shelter, they had tried to fly though his large front window.

The man felt sorry for the birds and tried to direct them to a barn in the back of his house. He opened the barn doors and turned on a light. But the birds would not come. The man scattered bread crumbs on the snow, making a trail from the front door to the stable entrance. Still the birds ignored him. He tried catching them, and then shooing at them. They only scattered.

Realizing the birds were frightened, he thought, *If only I can think of some way to make them trust me. If only I could be a bird, talk with them, speak their language. Then I could show them the way—so they could really hear and see and understand.*

About that time, the church bells began to ring. As he listened to the glad tidings of Christmas, the truth dawned. The man sank to his knees in the snow.

Just like those little frightened birds could only relate to another bird like themselves, God sent His Son Jesus to earth so that He could relate to us, and we to Him. The next time your friends are hurt or lonely and in need of someone to talk to, let them know that there is Someone to talk to, let them know that there is Someone who truly hears and sees and understands where they are and what they're going through.

That Someone is Jesus. ❖

Traditions for a Christ-Centered Christmas

PLANT NARCISSUS BULBS TO MARK THE FOUR WEEKS OF ADVENT.

Paperwhite narcissus are a beautiful way to mark the course of Advent. Select firm, shiny, brown-coated bulbs at a nursery or garden center. Most of the narcissus bulb stock that reaches the United States comes from Israel where the climate offers perfect growing conditions. These strains are called "Galilea," "Ziva," "Bethlehem," and "Nazareth"—an interesting tie-in to the Christmas season.

Just before the beginning of Advent, plant the bulbs either in bowls of pebbles or pots with soil. If you want to use gravel, fill the container about two-thirds full with gravel, settle the bulb with about one-half the bulb covered, and add water just to the level of the top of the gravel. If using pots with soil—considered the best method—use ordinary potting soil and small pots about five inches in diameter. Fill the pot to about two-thirds full. Settle the bulbs firmly in the wet soil, and add more soil to cover. Leave about one inch of bulb and emerging shoot uncovered. Water thoroughly. One five-inch pot will hold three to four bulbs. Let each family member settle a bulb in the pot. The result will be a beautiful narcissus bouquet.

After planting, place in a cool, light area indoors. Keep the narcissus watered, not allowing them to dry out. Shoots will turn green and lengthen. Buds emerge in about three weeks and full blooms in four weeks—a beautiful, living complement to your Advent celebration.

Reflection

⚜

Ah! Dearest Jesus, Holy Child,

Make thee a bed, soft, undefiled,

Within my heart, that it may be

A quiet chamber kept for thee.

MARTIN LUTHER

The Story of the Christ Child

[READING FROM LUKE 1:29–33 MSG]

She [Mary] *was thoroughly shaken, wondering what was behind a greeting like that. But the angel assured her, "Mary, you have nothing to fear. God has a surprise for you: You will become pregnant and give birth to a son and call his name Jesus.*

> *He will be great,*
> *be called 'Son of the Highest.'*
> *The Lord God will give him*
> *the throne of his father David;*
> *He will rule Jacob's house forever—*
> *no end, ever, to his kingdom."*

*H*ave you ever considered what you would do if confronted by an angel as Mary was? This young girl, probably a teenager, must have been quite astonished to see an archangel in front of her. *Surely*, she must have thought, *such appearances are made only in the temple and only to the important religious leaders*. But here he was, talking to her.

God is sovereign. He uses who He chooses to fulfill His purposes on the earth. His criteria are simple. He looks for eyes that are open to see Him and hearts that are open to receive Him. He looks for those who have courage to do as He asks. God knew Mary's heart. He knew she would listen, surrender, and obey.

Can God depend on you in the same way He knew He could depend on Mary? Why or why not?

[Jesus said,] *"Blessed are the pure in heart,*
for they will see God."
MATTHEW 5:8

Dear Lord:

As I reflect on it, I am amazed by Mary's story. She must have had no real inkling why You would choose her for the role she was about to play. And yet, she humbly acknowledged and accepted Your plan with all of her heart. She even did so with grace, humility, and enthusiasm. I want to be more like her—someone who is open to your purposes even when I cannot understand all that is at stake. I want to be surrendered to Your holy will, knowing that You have prepared me for any assignment You might make. Thank You for the honor and privilege of being used by You.

Amen.

"Chief Cornerstone"

⁂

Consequently, you are no longer foreigners and aliens,
but fellow citizens with God's people and members of
God's household, built on the foundation of the
apostles and prophets, with Christ Jesus himself
as the chief cornerstone.
EPHESIANS 2:19-20

THE BIBLE CALLS JESUS the *chief cornerstone*. In terms of architecture, this stone would be the pivotal stone upon which everything rests. In like manner, Jesus is the pivotal point between God and humankind. When we accept Christ, He becomes the foundation of our relationship with God. Our lives become stable and secure in Him.

When Mary said yes to God's plan to bear the Christ Child, she was actually playing a part in this heavenly building project. She would give birth to the One who would become the *chief cornerstone*.

Something to Remember

Grandma came from the "old country." She spoke with a thick accent and often struggled to find the right English words when she shared about her faith in God. But Grandma could cook! And when Christmastime came around, Grandma's house was filled with the delicious aroma of her Christmas breads and rolls.

As the years passed, Grandma succumbed to painful arthritis in her hands and shoulders. Though she could no longer knead the dough used in her Christmas rolls, Grandma still could share her faith.

One year Grandma asked her granddaughter to come for a visit. Grandma wanted to make her Christmas rolls one last time. Using the granddaughter's hands and Grandma's expertise, the two women worked together, kneading the dough and stuffing the rolls while Grandma kept saying, "Remember this ... do this."

That night, before she went to sleep, the granddaughter carefully wrote down all of the ingredients and reviewed all the steps in making Grandma's rolls so that she could remember how to make them the following year. And she did. And she still does. Now every Christmas she teaches her children and grandchildren how to make Grandma's Christmas rolls, filling her kitchen with the same delicious aroma that filled her grandma's kitchen long ago.

But the granddaughter shares more than a recipe and special Christmas rolls to feed her hungry family. She also shares Grandma's lessons of faith and trust in God.

Grandma's rolls may fill an empty stomach, but Grandma's faith could fill an empty heart. Now that's something to remember! ✤

The Story of the Christ Child

[READING FROM LUKE 1:34-35 MSG]

Mary said to the angel, "But how? I've never slept with a man."

The angel answered,
"The Holy Spirit will come upon you,
the power of the Highest hover over you;
Therefore, the child you bring to birth
will be called Holy, Son of God."

*I*t seems surprising, but Mary, that young teenage girl, had the courage to ask questions of the Lord. She asked Him how a virgin could possibly give birth to a child. Her boldness was rewarded. In simple, human terms, God explained to her how the incarnation of His Son would take place.

Do you have questions of the Lord? Ask them. He will answer them, perhaps not as you expect or as you hope, but you can be sure that His answers will be enough—enough to get you on the way to His will, enough to light the path ahead. Don't let questions keep you from obeying God's will for your life. Ask them and move forward.

What is the most pressing question you want to ask God? Are you ready to receive His answer?

Call to me and I will answer you and tell you great and unsearchable things you do not know.
JEREMIAH 33:3

Dear Lord:

No wonder Mary was Your choice—so humble and yet so bold. I wonder if she spent time alone reflecting on what was happening to her—the changes in her body, Joseph's unexpected response to her situation, the words the angel had spoken to her. Her understanding was so small and yet her faith was so big. Help me to find the courage to bring all my questions to You, Lord, knowing that You will hear me and respond. I promise to listen and reflect on Your answers, drawing from them the understanding I need to give You the gift of myself and meet each day with joy and enthusiasm.

Amen.

"Alpha and Omega"

[Jesus said,] *"See, I am coming soon; my reward is with me, to repay according to everyone's work. I am the Alpha and the Omega, the first and the last, the beginning and the end."*
REVELATION 22:12–13 NRSV

SO MUCH ABOUT GOD is a mystery—unsolvable by our limited human brains. We simply can't comprehend Him. He is too great for us on every level. The Bible does give us glimpses though—glimpses of His character, His reasoning, His great love. And we know one other thing. God *is* and *was* and always *will be*. He is *Alpha*—the beginning, the first—and *Omega*, the ending, the last. He truly has the big picture because His consciousness spans eternity. Jesus lived thirty-three years on this earth. His human body was bound by time. But this was just a point in time for Jesus, God's Son, for whom there was no beginning and will be no end.

A Birthday Party for Jesus

How would you feel if you had a birthday party and the people attending gave presents to one another but not to you?

That's the question Mable Dumas addressed at her prayer group's holiday party. As the ladies arrived in her home, she served refreshments and then said, "Ladies, we like to visit with one another, but from this point on, let's talk only about Jesus. He is our guest of honor, and it's His birthday."

As the women gathered around the fireplace, Mable sat on the hearth and led a conversation about Jesus. The focal point became a wooden nativity set.

The ladies discussed everything from Gabriel's visit to Mary to the astonishing moment when God became so small for our sakes—our Savior, lying on a clump of hay.

Then Mable announced, "Every birthday party has gifts. Now it's time for us to give our gifts to Jesus." She passed around a basket filled with tiny, decorated boxes. At the appointed time, each participant opened her box in an attitude of prayer and read aloud a Scripture, along with the companion "gift" to place on an altar. These included such things as:

My heart
My faith
My future
My dreams

During the touching, intimate moment, several women moved to a kneeling position and then wept softly. That day became special because the ladies chose to give Jesus the most meaningful gift of all: *themselves*.

The Story of the Christ Child

[READING FROM LUKE 1:36–38 MSG]

"And did you know that your cousin Elizabeth conceived a son, old as she is? Everyone called her barren, and here she is six months pregnant! Nothing, you see, is impossible with God."

And Mary said,

"Yes, I see it all now:

I'm the Lord's maid, ready to serve.

Let it be with me

just as you say."

Then the angel left her.

*M*ary got her questions answered before the angel left her. She also firmly established her willingness to do all God had planned for her. She would become completely submissive to His will.

Her willingness never wavered—not when she was misunderstood by neighbors and family, not when she was asked to lift her pregnant body onto the back of a donkey and travel for days to an unfamiliar destination, not when she gave birth in a stable, not when she and Joseph had to flee to Egypt in order to protect the child's life. Instead of complaining about her situation, she chose instead to reflect on the goodness and greatness of God. She thought it a privilege to be part of God's eternal drama. Her heart was settled. She trusted that the One who had initiated the plan and invited her to be a part of it would provide all that she needed.

Can you trust God to provide all you need? Have you settled in your heart that He is going to care for you?

Let us not become weary in doing good, for at the proper time we will reap a harvest if we do not give up.
GALATIANS 6:9

Dear Lord:

Who wouldn't admire Mary's resolve—all the hardships she encountered and yet she never whined or fussed or wavered in her determination to be faithful to the instructions she had been given. I know, Lord, that I would not be so. I would be asking "why this" and "why that," wondering about each situation along the way. In my heart though, I desire to trust You in the same way Mary did. Strengthen me to play my role in Your eternal drama without whining, without complaining, without hesitating. Help me to trust in Your goodness and greatness—just like Mary did.

Amen.

"I Am"

The Jews said to him, "You are not yet fifty years old, and have you seen Abraham?" Jesus said to them, "Very truly, I tell you, before Abraham was, I am."
JOHN 8:57-58 NRSV

NO OTHER PEOPLE KNEW more hardship than the Israelites as they traveled in the wilderness in search of the Promised Land. It could be argued that they brought much of the hardship on themselves. But God loved them despite their failings. In an effort to console His people and still their anxiety, God told them simply and emphatically, "I AM who I AM!" (Exodus 3:14). If you need food, I am your provision. If you need comfort, I am your consolation. If you have questions, I am your wisdom and counsel. By calling Himself the "I Am," Jesus identified Himself as part of the Godhead and all they would ever need. He was the I Am for Mary and Joseph, for the shepherds and the wise men. And He is the *I Am* for us today.

Life's Ups and Downs

The highlight of every Christmas season was the trip to Uncle Bill's farm. Uncle Bill was a dairyman. Though he kept only a small herd, Uncle Bill's life revolved around the rhythms of farm life—early morning milkings, chores, machinery repair, but also, fun! After a good snowfall, Uncle Bill would hitch his horse to an old box wagon equipped with a pair of horse sled runners. All of the visiting relatives would pile into the wagon. Then Uncle Bill would snap the reins, and off they'd go, cold wind painting their faces red, whistles and laughter echoing over the countryside.

Sometimes the wagon would slide around a bend and get stuck in a snowdrift. Then Uncle Bill would make everyone get out of the wagon. Someone would have to hold the horse's head while everyone else pushed. If anyone complained, Uncle Bill would remind him or her that you have to take the bad along with the good in life. Before they knew it, the wagon would be sledding down the road again with everyone whistling and laughing all the way home.

Uncle Bill knew that while good times are an occasion for happiness, bad times are a time to be content, not a time to moan, fret, or worry. God is still in control. We can trust Him, and soon, like the old sled wagon, everything will be back on track, and we'll be whistling and laughing all the way home. ❖

The Story of the Christ Child

[READING FROM LUKE 1:39-42 MSG]

BLESSED AMONG WOMEN

Mary didn't waste a minute. She got up and traveled to a town in Judah in the hill country, straight to Zachariah's house, and greeted Elizabeth. When Elizabeth heard Mary's greeting, the baby in her womb leaped. She was filled with the Holy Spirit, and sang out exuberantly.

*N*ot only does God have a plan for your life, not only is He willing to answer your questions about that plan, but when He hears you state that plan with your words, He is quick to confirm His purpose. Mary rushed to see Elizabeth, anxious to tell her what the angel had said to her. But when she arrived, another surprise was awaiting her—Elizabeth spontaneously confirmed the angel's message.

God will always confirm His instructions to you. He knows that your senses are human and fallible. If God has spoken to you, wait for His confirmation. It will come—probably from a source you can trust in, but maybe in a way you do not expect. The last thing He wants is for you to move in the wrong direction, waste your time, and miss your true purpose. Submit yourself to the Lord, and He will send you the confirmation you need.

Are you willing to wait for God to confirm His instructions to you?

*Trust in the L*ORD *with all your heart*
and lean not on your own understanding;
in all your ways acknowledge him,
and he will make your paths straight.
PROVERBS 3:5-6

Dear Lord:

Keep me from pursuing paths that are simply exten-
sions of my own mental processes and imagination. I know
Your purposes are based in reality and in fact. I will be waiting for Your confirmation, the assurance I need that I am
pointed in the right direction and taking the proper steps
to achieve Your will in my life. I believe that as I wait and
watch, you will be working in my heart to make me more
determined to pursue Your purposes rather than my own.
Thank You for Your promise to walk with me every step of
the path You have chosen for me.

Amen.

"The Door"

❖

[Jesus said,] *"I am the door: by me if any man enter in, he shall be saved, and shall go in and out, and find pasture."*
JOHN 10:9 KJV

LIKE ANYTHING ELSE, we enter the kingdom of God through the door—and Jesus says that He is that door, the only door in fact. Even before God's purpose for our lives is revealed, one thing must be secured—we must be under His dominion. His first and primary purpose for our lives is that we receive forgiveness for our sins and be restored to fellowship with our heavenly Father. Only then can we become the people He created us to be. Jesus is the One who provided the gift of forgiveness, so He is the door. No one else, no matter how noble or wise, can do that for us. He alone lived a perfect life. He alone met God's standards. He alone died for us. He alone is *The Door.*

Faithful Saints

Rev. B. C. Housewright, a retired minister, and his wife, Lottie, exited their car and began an arduous walk to the worship center. B. C. leaned on his cane and walked with a limp; he had recently been diagnosed with cancer. Lottie, bending forward, suffering with osteoporosis and other health problems, placed her hand on B. C.'s arm for stability. This couple, married for more than fifty-five years, had every reason to excuse themselves from attending church. But as long as they could, they came—jovial and overflowing with love, thankfulness, and enthusiasm for the Lord.

Two elderly people met Mary and Joseph when they brought Jesus to the temple in Jerusalem to be dedicated to God.

Simeon, a devout Jewish man, expected the Messiah to appear. The Scripture says, "The Holy Spirit was upon him" (Luke 2:25), and with that preview of Pentecost, Simeon scooped up Baby Jesus into his arms and prophesied over the child. He knew the Messiah had come.

Anna, widowed after only seven years of marriage, had served in the temple for many years. When she saw the infant, she too recognized Him in her heart. Anna began worshipping and thanking God.

How uplifting these two affirming experiences must have been for young Mary and Joseph. �֍

The Story of the Christ Child

[READING FROM LUKE 1:42-45 MSG]

[Elizabeth] sings out:
"You're so blessed among women,
*   and the babe in your womb, also blessed!*
And why am I so blessed that
*   the mother of my Lord visits me?*
The moment the sound of your
*   greeting entered my ears,*
The babe in my womb
*   skipped like a lamb for sheer joy.*
Blessed woman, who believed what God said,
*   believed every word would come true!"*

*I*t seems that Mary and Elizabeth were celebrating. They were excited to be part of God's purpose and plan. The barren woman and the young virgin were filled with joy to know they had been chosen by God to do His bidding.

You will be celebrating as well when you realize that God has chosen you. You may not be the mother of the one who would announce the arrival of the Messiah or the one who would give birth to the Christ Child, but God's plan for you is important and unique. Thank Him for the role He has chosen for you to play in His eternal drama of love and redemption.

Are you celebrating the role God has given you?

I want you to get out there and walk—better yet, run!—on the road God called you to travel.... You have one Master, one faith, one baptism, one God and Father of all, who rules over all, works through all, and is present in all....

But that doesn't mean you should all look and speak and act the same. Out of the generosity of Christ, each of us is given his own gift.
EPHESIANS 4:1, 5-7 MSG

Dear Lord:

I lift up my voice in praise for Your everlasting love that turned us from despair to eternal hope. It amazes me to think that long before You created the first man and the first woman, You knew that they would choose to rebel against Your love and care. Before any of it happened, You came up with a solution. You would provide a way for them to come back to You. Thank You for your amazing plan. And thank You for allowing me the privilege to play a part in it. I rejoice in the role You have given me.

Amen.

"Lamb of God"

❄

The next day he [John the Baptist] *saw Jesus coming toward him and declared, "Here is the Lamb of God who takes away the sin of the world!"*
JOHN 1:29 NRSV

IN THE ETERNAL DRAMA God conceived in His relationship with humankind, Jesus plays the primary role. You could say that He is the star of that production. Though He was God the Son, Jesus would allow Himself to be born as a human being, live a perfect life here among us, and then die a terrible death to pay for our sin and rebellion. To prepare the hearts of His people, God instituted the concept of sacrifice for sin long before Jesus came. He instructed His people to kill a lamb to atone for their sins. This served as a "make do" solution until it was time to send Jesus to be the final sacrifice—once and for all. Jesus played His part in the eternal drama flawlessly. He was and is and always will be—the *Lamb of God.*

Unexpected Solo

Virginia finished her lines and walked slowly on to the "Christmas on Main Street" stage. The rest of the "Ringer/Singer" choir was to join her to sing and ring handbells. Virginia took her place with much more poise than was usual for a five-year-old.

The cue came for the choir to join Virginia. She looked left toward the stage door. Nothing happened. Her gaze went to her choir director on the front row. He nodded at her to begin. *Begin?* She thought. *But where are the others?*

Virginia's stomach was full of butterflies. Her eyes brimmed with tears. She was on stage before a thousand people. Alone. But the show must go on. Silently she asked God to help her. She began to sing, softly at first but then with more confidence. Her lone handbell resonated at just the right moment. Slowly her mouth curved into a smile. She was actually enjoying being a star.

Halfway through the song, the rest of the choir rushed in. They had been given the wrong time to enter from backstage. Getting to their spots *quickly* seemed more important than getting to their spots *quietly*! Together they sang and rang the last few lines of "Ring the Bells."

Virginia never planned to sing a solo. At the performance the night before, everything had gone perfectly. The choir appeared on time and joined Virginia on stage. The audience had loved these twelve musically accomplished children.

Although the choir messed up at this performance, Virginia knew what was expected of her, and she didn't let the unexpected situation bother her. Wise beyond her years, she took her cue and sang. With God's help, she learned courage and confidence. ❖

The Story of the Christ Child

[READING FROM LUKE 1:46–56 MSG]

Mary said,
"I'm bursting with God-news;
I'm dancing the song of my Savior God.
God took one good look at me,
and look what happened—
I'm the most fortunate woman on earth!
What God has done for me will never be forgotten,
the God whose very name is holy,
set apart from all others.
His mercy flows in wave after wave
on those who are in awe before him.
He bared his arm and showed his strength,
scattered the bluffing braggarts.
He knocked tyrants off their high horses,
pulled victims out of the mud.
The starving poor sat down to a banquet;
the callous rich were left out in the cold.
He embraced his chosen child, Israel;
he remembered and piled on the mercies,
piled them high.
It's exactly what he promised,
beginning with Abraham and right up to now."

Mary stayed with Elizabeth for three months and then
went back to her own home.

$\mathcal{A}$T THE TIME of Christ's birth, God's people Israel were beaten down and subdued. They were oppressed not only by the brutal Roman regime but also by their own religious leaders. Their hearts were crying out for God to rescue them. Where was the Messiah, God had promised? Mary and Elizabeth were celebrating not only God's favor in their own lives but also His favor on their people—Israel.

God's plan for your life is part of His plan for humanity as a whole. He is rescuing you that you might join His effort to rescue others. His intention is for none to perish. When you reflect on this, it makes all the difference in the world in how You respond to His call.

Did you know that God has poured out His favor on your life? How can you share that favor with others?

But in your hearts set apart Christ as Lord.
Always be prepared to give an answer to everyone who
asks you to give the reason for the hope that you have.
1 PETER 3:15

Dear Lord:

Thank You for pouring out Your favor in my life, for rescuing me from the mess I had made of things, and putting me on the path to eternal life. Help me remember that You have honored me with the responsibility of celebrating Your redemption before the eyes of the world. May I always treat that responsibility soberly and respectfully. Show me how to live in a way that is pleasing to You so that those who know me will want to know the source of joy and righteousness that fills my life.

Amen.

"Light of the World"

When Jesus spoke again to the people, he said, "I am the light of the world. Whoever follows me will never walk in darkness, but will have the light of life."
JOHN 8:12

WHEN THE FIRST MAN, Adam, and the first woman, Eve, sinned against God, their spirits turned dark and died within them. But God had no intention of abandoning those whom He had created in His own image. He would restore the life and light to the souls of men now shrouded in darkness. He would pay the penalty for Adam's sin—spiritual darkness and death—by providing a fitting sacrifice, the pure and holy life of His Son, Jesus, who would literally become the *Light of the World*. All those who received Jesus would receive forgiveness of sins and spiritual rebirth. Jesus was more than a babe in a manger. He was the physical promise that the light of life would once again illuminate our hearts.

Festival of Lights

The menorah, a candelabra with four candles on each side and one in the middle, actually represents a miracle. It is used during the winter Jewish holiday know as Hanukkah or The Festival of Lights. Hanukkah, which means *dedication*, commemorates the revolt against the Syrian Greeks in 167–164 BC, when the Jews recaptured the temple and rededicated it to God's service.

The Greeks had extinguished the great seven-branched candelabra in the temple, and only enough oil remained for the light to burn one day. It took eight days for the priests to consecrate more oil. Nevertheless, the Jews lit the lampstand, and it continued to burn for eight full days.

Thus the Feast of Dedication, also called the Festival of Lights, was established. In Jewish homes the miniature menorah candles are lit, one each day, to represent the eight days. The center candle is the *shamash*, a Hebrew word meaning *servant*, and it is used to light the other candles. From Scripture, Christians know Jesus is the Light of the World, God's *shamash*.[2]

The Jerusalem temple has been destroyed, but when we receive Christ, we become the temple of God and the *shamash* shines in our hearts. We become lights in a dark world. Through His Holy Spirit we have a never-ending supply of oil to keep our lamps brightly burning. ✤

Traditions for a Christ-Centered Christmas

CREATE A "JESSE TREE."

The Jesse Tree comes from Isaiah 11:1: "A shoot will come up from the stump of Jesse; from his roots a Branch will bear fruit." The word "branch" in this context denotes newness and encouragement. It alludes to Jesus Christ, the expected Messiah. (See Jeremiah 23:5.)

The Jesse Tree is a way to tell the story of God in the Old Testament and connect the Advent season with the faithfulness of God throughout history. Though an actual tree can be used, most people prefer a banner or poster on a wall. This can be plain or as elaborate as you would like to make it. It can be made from heavy felt or cotton, the design can be embroidered, appliquéd, stitched, or created with markers. Let your imagination lead the way. The background should be purple or blue (the colors of Advent).

Choose a story from the Bible (Old and New Testaments) for each day of Advent. Then as a family create symbols for those stories. These can be made with construction paper and markers or cut from magazines. Old Christmas cards are a good source of appropriate symbols. Each day of the Advent season, read a story (in sequence) and ask a family member to attach the appropriate ornament to the banner with pins or Velcro.

Commitment

~❧~

To travel the road to Bethlehem is to
keep a rendezvous with wonder, to
answer the call of wisdom, and to
bow the knee in worship.

JOHN A. KNIGHT

The Story of the Christ Child

[READING FROM LUKE 1:57–66 MSG]

THE BIRTH OF JOHN

When Elizabeth was full-term in her pregnancy, she bore a son. Her neighbors and relatives, seeing that God had overwhelmed her with mercy, celebrated with her.

On the eighth day, they came to circumcise the child and were calling him Zachariah after his father. But his mother intervened: "No. He is to be called John."

"But," they said, "no one in your family is named that." They used sign language to ask Zachariah what he wanted him named.

Asking for a tablet, Zachariah wrote, "His name is to be John." That took everyone by surprise. Surprise followed surprise—Zachariah's mouth was now open, his tongue loose, and he was talking, praising God!

A deep, reverential fear settled over the neighborhood, and in all that Judean hill country people talked about nothing else. Everyone who heard about it took it to heart, wondering, "What will become of this child? Clearly, God has his hand in this."

*I*t's almost a certainty that when you begin to follow the will and purpose of God for your life, some people will think you have taken leave of your senses. The Bible tells us that the ways of God are foolishness to the world (1 Cor. 2:14). Zachariah and Elizabeth encountered this kind of opposition. God had instructed them to name their son John. But the custom of the day was to name a son after his father. They didn't hesitate to do what God had said. It was an act of obedience for Zachariah, and when he had done the right thing, his tongue was loosed.

Let everything you do in this Advent season and in the rest of the year to come, be done in obedience to God, no matter what others might think, say, or do. God's purposes transcend the customs of men. The peace in your heart will tell you that you've done the right thing.

Have you ever encountered opposition when you tried to do what you felt God was asking you to do?

Am I now trying to win the approval of men, or of God?
Or am I trying to please men?
GALATIANS 1:10

Dear Lord:

It's hard not to listen to those around me. Everybody seems to have an opinion these days. Even straightforward choices concerning honesty and fidelity and helping others are often second-guessed. I'm sure that there will be plenty of people who will second-guess anything I try to do for You. Give me the courage, I pray, to stand strong, unwavering— like Zachariah and Elizabeth—and carry out Your purpose for my life, one instruction at a time. It's more important to me to be pleasing to You than to have the favor of everyone I know. Thank You for Your goodness and graciousness to me.

Amen.

"The Way, the Truth, and the Life"

Jesus answered, "I am the way and the truth and the life. No one comes to the Father except through me."
JOHN 14:6

WHEN JESUS—God Incarnate—walked here on earth, there was much confusion about who should be worshipped and where, how to live life and why. The religious leaders of the day made things worse by arguing openly over the matters of doctrine, the Law, and the interpretation of Old Testament Scripture. Jesus put an end to the confusion by making a simple statement: I am *the Way, the Truth, and the Life*. Everything they needed to know—every question and every answer—was resident in Him. Today, there are more questions than ever—doctrines, religions, denominations all vying for attention. But now as then, Jesus' statement stands unshaken. He is the Way to God, the Bearer of eternal Truth, and the Giver of eternal Life.

A Change of Direction

Two couples on vacation rented a car to drive on the back roads of beautiful British Columbia. Jim and Fran sat in the front, and Fran's mother, Billie, and her step-dad, Dobber, sat in the back.

Jim was driving along when they saw a dirt road angling to the right with the correct highway number posted. Fran said, "Surely that isn't the main road. Maybe the sign was turned. Look, the road straight ahead is paved and lined with utility poles, too."

After a lighthearted discussion, the couples took a vote and decided to stay on what appeared to be the main highway. After a few miles, Jim drove up a little hill, and then suddenly all they could see was water, a few small buildings, and a campground sign. The road came to a dead end there at a lovely lake and campsite. The couples began laughing as Jim wheeled the car around and headed back to the dirt road turn they had missed. Eventually, the humble highway meandered into the most magnificent scenery of all.

At Christmastime, we could stay on the broad, paved road and mindlessly travel to the dead end of shopping, tinsel, and plastic. Or we could, like the shepherds, change our thinking and our plans, turn down the narrow road to Bethlehem, and worship the newborn King. Which will you choose? ❖

The Story of the Christ Child

[READING FROM LUKE 1:67-75 MSG]

Then Zachariah was filled with the Holy Spirit and prophesied,

"Blessed be the Lord, the God of Israel;
he came and set his people free.
He set the power of salvation
in the center of our lives,
and in the very house of David his servant,
Just as he promised long ago
through the preaching of his holy prophets:
Deliverance from our enemies
and every hateful hand;
Mercy to our fathers,
as he remembers to do what he said he'd do,
What he swore to our father Abraham—
a clean rescue from the enemy camp,
So we can worship him
without a care in the world,
made holy before him as long as we live."

*W*ith obedience comes blessing and freedom and power and understanding. These are the things Zachariah received when he committed to doing the Lord's bidding, despite the objections of others. He was blessed to have played a role in God's eternal plan of redemption, free from the constraints of tradition and disbelief, empowered by the Holy Spirit, and filled with understanding of God's plan for the redemption of humankind.

Many times we run from obedience. We think it will limit us, require us to do what we don't want to do. But, as Zachariah learned, it will have the opposite effect in our lives. We will be liberated and empowered. Obeying God is not an obstacle but a privilege.

Do you believe that God still rewards obedience and commitment to His purpose? In what ways?

If ye be willing and obedient,
ye shall eat the good of the land.
ISAIAH 1:19 KJV

Dear Lord:

Knowing what I know, which is much more than Zachariah knew in his time, it should be easy for me to see that Your purpose for my life is my only path to success, satisfaction, and fulfillment. Help me keep that always in the forefront of my thinking, always believing that Your way is best for me. I am so small, so powerless, but You have given me a kite string with which to sail high above my own limited abilities and become part of what You are doing. Help me to say yes to all you ask of me.

Amen.

"Lord of Glory"

We speak of God's secret wisdom, a wisdom that has been hidden and that God destined for our glory before time began. None of the rulers of this age understood it, for if they had, they would not have crucified the Lord of glory.

1 CORINTHIANS 2:7-8

THE BIBLE TEACHES THAT when Jesus left heaven, was born as a human child, grew up, and ministered God's love to humankind, and was crucified, He brought glory to God, His Father (John 14:13). Many who saw Him crucified thought just the opposite. There on the cross was a mortal man, executed as a criminal, and doomed. They did not know what Jesus knew, what God knew—He would soon burst from the tomb, victorious over sin and death. They did not know that He was destined to become both the crucified king and the *Lord of Glory*. Jesus is no longer in the manger, no longer on the cross. He has risen, and His glory is now apparent to all.

Keep Your Eyes on Him

Ginger ran to her mother's room as fast as her five-year-old legs would take her. "Come look; come quick," she squealed.

"What is it, honey?" her mother asked.

"You have to come see."

Ginger grabbed Mother by the hand and led her to the living room. Stopping in front of the credenza, Ginger pointed her chubby little finger to the manger scene.

When Mother had arranged the figures the previous night, the display was properly balanced and evenly spaced. The larger figures were near the stable, and the smaller ones were at the far edge of the walnut top so as to achieve proper perspective. Mother had been pleased with the visual picture. Now the figures were clustered under the stable roof. Each stood facing the manger, as close as possible to the Baby Jesus.

"Isn't that better? Now they can all see," Ginger proudly exclaimed.

"See?" asked her puzzled mother.

"Yes, see," said Ginger. "When I got up, all the men were scattered around. Some of them were so far away that they couldn't see Baby Jesus. I moved them closer so they could see Him."

Can you see Jesus, or do you need to move a little closer to the manger this season in order to see the Savior? ❖

DAY 17

The Story of the Christ Child

[READING FROM LUKE 1:76–80 MSG]

Zachariah … prophesied,
> *"And you, my child, 'Prophet of the Highest,'*
>> *will go ahead of the Master*
>> *to prepare his ways,*
> *Present the offer of salvation to his people,*
>> *the forgiveness of their sins.*
> *Through the heartfelt mercies of our God,*
>> *God's Sunrise will break in upon us,*
> *Shining on those in the darkness,*
>> *those sitting in the shadow of death,*
> *Then showing us the way, one foot at a time,*
>> *down the path of peace."*

The child grew up, healthy and spirited. He lived out in the desert until the day he made his prophetic debut in Israel.

*T*he Advent season presents many opportunities to teach your children about the love and mercy of God, just as Zachariah and Elizabeth did. What a wonderful blessing to grow up with an understanding of God's ways and a commitment to His purposes.

As you talk about the Christ Child lying in the manger, introduce your children to the healing Christ, the teaching Christ, the suffering Christ, the risen Christ, and the Christ who will receive them one day into glory. Children have a great capacity for understanding spiritual principles. Reach out to them, and ask God to help you raise them in an atmosphere of spiritual love and support.

Are you committed to presenting to your children both the baby in Bethlehem's manger and the risen Lord of glory?

Love GOD, your God, with your whole heart: love him with all that's in you, love him with all you've got!
Write these commandments that I've given you today on your hearts. Get them inside of you and then get them inside your children.
DEUTERONOMY 6:5-7 MSG

Dear Lord:

Help me this Advent season to teach my children about You. Give me good ideas that will convey the principles of Your kingdom. Thank You for the privilege of raising my children to know and love You. I want them all to know You, to love You, and to follow You. I want them to build their lives around You and receive the gift of salvation that You bring. This season give me the words to help them see past the manger to a man whose actions open the door for them to receive forgiveness of sins and eternal life.

Amen.

"Bread of Life"

❖

Jesus said to them, "I am the bread of life. Whoever
comes to me will never be hungry, and whoever
believes in me will never be thirsty."
JOHN 6:35 NRSV

AS THE ISRAELITES TRAVELED in the wilderness, God sustained
them by sending manna from heaven. It served as their daily
bread, providing them with the necessary nutrition to continue
on their journey. In the same way, Jesus is our spiritual bread,
providing the spiritual nutrition needed to sustain our souls. If
He had not been born in that tiny manger, we would not have
survived. And our very survival depends on Him still. As we
acknowledge His sacrifice and partake of His victory, we are
saved. He is the *Bread of Life*. We must all grow in our understanding that He is more than Bethlehem's baby; He is also the
sustainer of our lives here on earth and the key to eternal life.

The Twelve Days of Giving

Patricia Moss listened to her children whine and cry in the toy department over which toy they'd get at Christmas and watched the pushing and shoving of the department store crowds. Then she stepped back for a minute to examine her family's values.

She decided to adopt a friend's tradition originating from the song, "The Twelve Days of Christmas." Beginning early in fall, she would try to pick a family that might need encouragement to get into the Christmas spirit. Then twelve days before Christmas, she and her family would begin slipping anonymous gifts onto the front porch of that family. They would write cute poems to go with the gifts, such as, "Twelve days before Christmas, a true friend gave to me, twelve candy canes, to hang upon the tree." The eleventh day before Christmas might be eleven fancy bows, the tenth day, a tin of ten giant homemade cookies, on and on right up to Christmas day.

One year the Moss family chose an elderly man who had suffered a stroke. He and his wife had decided not to put up a tree that year—that is, until the "twelve days" gifts started arriving. Another year they selected two families to cheer because both sons had friends whose families needed their love and care.

Patricia said that even after her sons were grown and had moved away, they still participated in this tradition when they returned home for Christmas.[3]

Patricia taught her children well, allowing them a hands-on opportunity not only to *see* good, but also to *do* good, moving them beyond their own problems as they gave generously of themselves to others. ❖

The Story of the Christ Child

[READING FROM LUKE 2:1–7 MSG]

THE BIRTH OF JESUS

*About that time Caesar Augustus ordered a census to
be taken throughout the Empire. This was the first
census when Quirinius was governor of Syria.
Everyone had to travel to his own ancestral home-
town to be accounted for. So Joseph went from the
Galilean town of Nazareth up to Bethlehem in Judah,
David's town, for the census. As a descendant of
David, he had to go there. He went with Mary, his
fiancée, who was pregnant.*

*While they were there, the time came for her
[Mary] to give birth. She gave birth to a son, her first-
born. She wrapped him in a blanket and laid him in a
manger, because there was no room in the hostel.*

*J*esus, the baby in Bethlehem's manger, was royalty to the highest degree. And yet … God required Joseph and Mary, the baby's mother, to be subjected to a harsh and inconvenient mandate of earthly government. On a whim Caesar Augustus decided to conduct a census, and the family was required to leave their home and travel a long distance. Are we to understand that even the King of Kings is subject to earthly authority?

A close look at Jesus' life shows that He never subverted authority. He challenged it, engaged it, but never overruled it—not even from the cross. His was a spiritual kingdom—his mission to rule in the hearts of men rather than hold sway over nations. Could He have been born in quarters fitting for a king? Yes, of course. But still He chose Bethlehem's manger. He conquered all, not by exercising His power but by submitting Himself to earthly authority and even death. Praise His Name!

Why do you think Jesus made Himself subject to earthly authority?

"My kingdom," said Jesus, "doesn't consist of what you see around you. If it did, my followers would fight so that I wouldn't be handed over to the Jews. But I'm not that kind of king, not the world's kind of king."

JOHN 18:36 MSG

Dear Lord:

So many things in Your kingdom seem to be upside-down. You are the king of all and yet You demanded nothing and made Yourself subject to the authority of earthly kings and magistrates. I know that You did that in order to carry out Your mission—to die as a sacrifice for my sins and the sins of all humankind. It seems like somewhere along the line, You would have said, "Okay, that's enough," and given Your persecutors a lesson they wouldn't forget. But You didn't. You stayed the course—for me! I don't know how to thank You for that or love You in return nearly as much as You have loved me. Accept my praise, dear Lord.

Amen.

"*King*"

Rejoice greatly, O daughter Zion!
Shout aloud, O daughter Jerusalem!
Lo, your king comes to you;
triumphant and victorious is he,
humble and riding on a donkey,
on a colt, the foal of a donkey.
ZECHARIAH 9:9 NRSV

THE DESIGNATION OF KING needs no explanation really. We all know that the king is a sovereign ruler. Jesus was proclaimed a *king* even as He lay in a manger. The angels announced it, the shepherds affirmed it, and the wise men acted on it by giving Him gifts fit for a king. Even the stars in the heavens bowed to His kingship. Many of His disciples believed that He had been sent to reign over an earthly kingdom, but that was not the case. Jesus came to reign over a spiritual kingdom—the kingdom of God. His subjects were the hearts and souls of men and women, over whom He rules with justice, truth, and loving-kindness.

Polished Thanks

As the pipe organ thundered out the notes to a favorite Christmas carol, stained-glass windows reflected the flickering of tiny candles at the church's Christmas Eve program. It should have put Maggie in the Christmas spirit, but all she could see was the dust and dirt and mess she would have to help clean up after this late-night service.

Maggie's grandfather was the church custodian. He needed extra help to keep the church clean at Christmastime, so Maggie and her siblings had been drafted to work with him. Trash would have to be collected, floors washed, and the white pews wiped clean of dirty handprints and boot marks before services the next day. Here Maggie was, stuck in an emptying church with a polishing cloth in her hand, wishing she could be anywhere else in the world. With a sigh she began to polish pews.

Grandpa noticed her work and said with a smile, "God must be hearing a lot of thanksgiving from you." When she didn't reply or look up from her polishing, Grandpa continued, "With every push of the broom or every shovel of snow, I thank God for my job, don't you?"

Maggie didn't want Grandpa to know that she was more resentful than thankful that night. But she knew in her heart that he was right. "I'm sorry, God," she muttered. And by the time Maggie finished polishing the row, she had found that she could thank God—even for a job polishing pews. The next morning, as the sun blazed through the colored windows and reflected off her polished pews, Maggie said "thanks" once more— and smiled. ❖

The Story of the Christ Child

[READING FROM LUKE 2:8–12 MSG]

AN EVENT FOR EVERYONE

There were sheepherders camping in the neighborhood. They had set night watches over their sheep. Suddenly, God's angel stood among them and God's glory blazed around them. They were terrified. The angel said, "Don't be afraid. I'm here to announce a great and joyful event that is meant for everybody, worldwide: A Savior has just been born in David's town, a Savior who is Messiah and Master. This is what you're to look for: a baby wrapped in a blanket and lying in a manger."

*C*an you imagine the terror the shepherds must have felt? Introverts, loners by nature, they suddenly found themselves surrounded by an amazing out-of-this-world production. We can be sure they had never seen anything like it in all their lives. But when the angel spoke to them with words of comfort, they listened to his words and were quieted. They received the angel's message.

Fear can keep you from becoming all God has created you to be. And yet, God has sent His Holy Spirit to whisper to your heart, "Don't be afraid." If you will hear Him, you will see wonders beyond anything you can imagine—just like the shepherds did. Much about our world is terrifying, but commit yourself to resisting fear. Receive courage from the Holy Spirit, and watch as God's redemption is played out on the grand stage.

What is your single greatest fear? What is keeping you from laying that fear at the feet of Jesus?

I will fear no evil,
for you are with me.
PSALM 23:4

Dear Lord:

When the shepherds saw the angels and heard their mighty chorus, they must have gasped with astonishment. Perhaps they shrank back and tried to hide themselves behind trees and boulders. But the angel preached a gospel of peace. He gave good news of a Savior. He calmed their fears and gave them a reason to be excited and hopeful. I want to know the peace that those shepherds felt that night, even in the face of such an extraordinary scene. I commit my fears to You. I come out from where I have been hiding. I am anxious to hear what You have to say and receive Your peace.

Amen.

"Prince of Peace"

Unto us a child is born, unto us a son is given: and the government shall be upon his shoulder: and his name shall be called Wonderful, Counselor, The mighty God, The everlasting Father, The Prince of Peace.

ISAIAH 9:6 KJV

GOD'S PEOPLE HAD KNOWN little peace in their existence, sometimes as a result of their own sinfulness. Beset by war, dominated, and enslaved, they were used to being oppressed. They looked to a day when the Messiah would come and bring peace to their lives. When the angel appeared along with the choir of the heavenly host, they were there to proclaim that the *Prince of Peace* had arrived. No longer would they be oppressed by sin, at war with themselves. They would be set free from guilt and shame, released to live in harmony with God. The shepherds did not know what would lie ahead for the young prince they found in a manger, but they knew enough. They knew He would change everything, and they would never be the same.

A Father's Hymn

History books record the suffering that befell families during the American Civil War. Many families were touched by the profound losses of life, damage to property, or reversals of fortune that accompanied the conflict.

Among the survivors of that dreadful war was a young man named Charley. When he left his home to serve as a soldier in the Union Army, Charley was convinced of his invincibility and emboldened by his ideals. But before the conflict was over, Charley returned home, wounded but alive. His arrival coincided with the beginnings of the Christmas holidays, and his father, Henry Wadsworth Longfellow, penned the lines of "I Heard the Bells on Christmas Day" in his honor.

Longfellow's words echo the cry of every heart that longs for peace on earth. And though this father's hymn reverberates with the heartache that accompanies the hardships of life, it ends with the assurance that God is not dead, and His peace will prevail.

I heard the bells on Christmas day,
Their old familiar carols play,
And wild and sweet the words repeat
Of peace on earth, good will to men.

And in despair I bowed my head
"There is no peace on earth," I said,
"For hate is strong and mocks the song
Of peace on earth, good will to men."

Then pealed the bells more loud and deep:
"God is not dead, nor doth He sleep;
The wrong shall fail, the right prevail
With peace on earth, good will to men."

The Story of the Christ Child

[READING FROM LUKE 2:13-18 MSG]

At once the angel was joined by a huge angelic choir singing God's praises:

> *"Glory to God in the heavenly heights,*
> *Peace to all men and women on earth who please him."*

As the angel choir withdrew into heaven, the sheepherders talked it over. "Let's get over to Bethlehem as fast as we can and see for ourselves what God has revealed to us." They left, running, and found Mary and Joseph, and the baby lying in the manger. Seeing was believing. They told everyone they met what the angels had said about this child. All who heard the sheepherders were impressed.

*W*e can only imagine what must have been going on in Mary's mind as she watched the parade of admirers pass by her child's manger crib. She knew this child was special, God's own child—the angel had told her that. But still, she must have been amazed by the drama unfolding before her.

Mary was wise. She took hold of her wonder as she watched the shepherds and the Magi deliver their gifts and tucked it away in her heart. She would need it later when things were unbearably difficult. She would experience intense suffering as a result of the horrors that lay ahead for her Son, but she would get through it. She would close her eyes and remember all that God had revealed concerning this child. This Son was not a mortal human being but the holy offspring of the Most High God. She had watched as the shepherds and the Magi brought confirmation to her heart. Her Son would redeem Israel. She was fully committed to the plan. She would not waver.

Do you trust God to keep His word to you even when you encounter painful circumstances and your dreams seem impossible?

I consider that our present sufferings are not worth comparing with the glory that will be revealed in us.
ROMANS 8:18

Dear Lord:

Mary was completely committed to You and to the purpose for which You called her. But her heart must have been breaking as she watched her Son suffer. She must have had to close her eyes and focus on what she knew—she had spoken with an angel, shepherds had bowed down to worship Him, Magi had traveled from afar with gifts for a king. These things comforted her through the worst a mother can endure. Show me how to tuck away the miracles I see in my daily life and the words you speak to my heart so that I will have them to hang onto in the hard times. Thank You for redeeming my life and my suffering and filling my heart with joy.

Amen.

"Redeemer"

*You will know that I, the L*ORD*, am your Savior, your*
Redeemer, the Mighty One of Jacob.... I will make
peace your governor and righteousness your ruler.
ISAIAH 60:16–17

IN ORDER FOR HUMANS to be royal children, set apart from
His other creations, God gave humankind a free will. They had
to be able to choose, and having chosen frivolously and improp-
erly, they had to be redeemed at any price. To redeem means to
recover a certain property by presenting a specific, appropriate
payment. God knew that the price would be high—the highest
that had ever been paid. Jesus' perfect life was that price of
redemption. He was the designated *Redeemer*. From the cradle
to the grave and then on to the shining glory of the resurrec-
tion, He performed His duties flawlessly, opening the door for all
who would choose to become part of His royal family.

Miracles Still Happen

A small preschooler waited impatiently as the long "North Pole" line snaked its way to the department store Santa. Finally, the child arrived at the head of the line. He climbed in Santa's lap, eager to express his wish list.

Santa's blue eyes twinkled as his burly arms wrapped around the young child. "And what do you want Santa to bring you?" he asked. "A toy truck? A new football? A bike?"

The little boy shook his head no. "I want a new daddy," he whispered.

"What do you mean, 'a new daddy'?"

"I want my daddy to act different. My daddy does drugs." A tear trickled down the preschooler's face.

Santa tried to console the child and promised his best, knowing he could not provide this impossible request.

Jim Cymbala, author of *Fresh Wind, Fresh Fire* and pastor of the inner city Brooklyn Tabernacle in New York, shows a video of one young man in his church. In that clip, the young man explains how he often left his wife and children for days, living in a literal doghouse while nurturing his crack addiction.

One night his wife and children had gone to Pastor Cymbala's church where many of the people began to pray earnestly for the woman's husband. That night, as if drawn by some unseen power, the young addict made his way to the church. As he walked down the aisle of the massive building, he heard his name spoken aloud in a petition to God. He knelt at the church altar and gave his life to Christ. He abandoned his habit and soon began singing in church and ministering to others.

Two stories—different endings. What seems impossible for us is always possible for God. Miracles still happen—and not just at Christmastime. ❖

Traditions for a Christ-Centered Christmas

BECOME CHRISTMAS ANGELS FOR ANOTHER FAMILY.

Emphasize a commitment of selfless giving by helping a family in the neighborhood who is struggling due to illness, death, or financial difficulty. Begin by teaching your children how to interact with those you are helping without causing them embarrassment. When you go shopping, ask each person to shop for a specific member of the family you are helping. Encourage your children to choose something on their own Christmas list. Resist the urge to let them buy one for themselves as well. In fact, it's a good idea for them not to receive that particular gift at all. This teaches the true meaning of sacrificial giving.

Ask each person to wrap his or her own gift and deliver them as a family. Make sure to call ahead.

Worship

What can I give Him,
   poor as I am?
If I were a shepherd,
   I would bring a lamb;
If I were a Wise Man,
   I would do my part;
Yet what can I give Him;
   give my heart.

CHRISTINA ROSSETTI

The Story of the Christ Child

[READING FROM LUKE 2:19–20 MSG]

Mary kept all these things to herself, holding them dear, deep within herself. The sheepherders returned and let loose, glorifying and praising God for everything they had heard and seen. It turned out exactly the way they'd been told!

The Nativity is, first and foremost, the threshold of redemption. The Christ must first come to earth, live as a human being—though without sin—and then die for the sins of humankind. Another theme embraces the story of the baby born in Bethlehem, however. It is the timeless story of worship. The angels worshipped, the Magi worshipped, the shepherds worshipped, even the simple barnyard animals were caught up in the glory all around them.

Worship is a primary theme of the Advent season as well. It is a time when our knees should bend in appreciation to the one who did so much for us. Worship of the quiet, introspective kind, and worship of the loud, celebrative kind are both acceptable to God. Give Him your thanks now and throughout the year to come.

In what ways can you worship God during this Advent season?

I urge you ... in view of God's mercy, to offer your bodies as living sacrifices, holy and pleasing to God—this is your spiritual act of worship.

ROMANS 12:1

Dear Lord:

As we come to the end of this Advent season, I want to open my heart to worship You in ways I have never worshipped before. I want to worship freely and completely, in ways that are worthy of Your goodness and greatness. Show me how to make my life a living sacrifice, pleasing in Your sight and representative of the awesome regard I have for You in my heart. Even now, Lord, I bow down on my knees and thank You for all You've done for me. I know that even with eternity before me, there will not be sufficient time to thank You enough, my gracious Savior, Redeemer, and Lord.

Amen.

"Savior"

Grow in the grace and knowledge of our Lord
and Savior Jesus Christ. To him be glory both
now and forever! Amen.
2 PETER 3:18

NOT ONLY DID JESUS redeem humankind in order to please His Father and provide royal sons and daughters for Him, but His pure, unblemished life and acts of sacrifice also serve to save us from an eternity separated from our Creator and from the fellowship He intended for us. Because He was willing to exchange His own life for ours, He has earned the title *Savior*. It best describes who He is in regard to us. Our poor choices led us away from God and doomed us to spiritual darkness, but Jesus entered our world as one of us and carved a path back to God with His own blood. He then lit the path with His own holiness. Because of Him, we can go home again.

Great Gift, Great Love

The story is told of a missionary who was once teaching a tribe in Africa about Christmas. "Christians," he said, "give gifts to others as an expression of their joy. In giving to others, they celebrate Christ's birthday and the gift that He is to mankind."

The missionary probably wondered if his teachings were clearly understood. He needn't have worried.

On Christmas morning, one of the natives presented the missionary with a beautiful seashell. When asked where he discovered such on extraordinary shell, the native said he had walked many miles to a certain bay, the only spot where such shells could be found.

"I think it was wonderful of you to travel so far to get this lovely gift for me," the teacher exclaimed.

His eyes brightening, the native replied, "Long walk, part of gift."[4]

In the familiar Christmas story *The Gift of the Magi*, a poor couple wanted to give each other a special gift. The woman decided to sell her beautiful, long hair, the pride of her life, to buy a fine watch chain for her husband's prized pocket watch. In the meantime, the husband, unaware of his wife's sacrifice, sold his watch to buy a set of beautiful, jeweled combs for his wife's hair. On Christmas day, they presented their selfless gifts, only to realize the irony of what they had done. They, too, might agree with the African student in their own words, "Big sacrifice, part of gift."

The greatest story of Christmas, the story that never grows old, the story that forever will be told, is that of a loving Father who gave His only Son as a gift to all—even to those who would never receive Him or appreciate the gift.

If asked why, perhaps God would answer, "Great love, part of gift." ❖

**DAY
23**

The Story of the Christ Child

[READING FROM LUKE 2:21–24 MSG]

BLESSINGS

When the eighth day arrived, the day of circumcision, the child was named Jesus, the name given by the angel before he was conceived.

Then when the days stipulated by Moses for purification were complete, they took him up to Jerusalem to offer him to God as commanded in God's Law: "Every male who opens the womb shall be a holy offering to God," and also to sacrifice the "pair of doves or two young pigeons" prescribed in God's Law.

$\mathcal{M}$ary and Joseph were careful to honor the religious law in every way concerning Jesus. Though they regarded Him as a child of royal birth, they took Him to Jerusalem where they offered Him back to God as required. Every ritual was carried out on His behalf. His adherence to every statute would be ensured. They were preparing Him for His mission—to become the sinless, holy Lamb of God who would once and for all fulfill the Law on behalf of every one of us.

We are not able to lead a sinless life—any attempt to do so would be futile. But because Jesus did for us what we could not do, we can now enjoy the fruits of His righteous life— having our sin erased and our future certain. As you worship the Christ Child, never forget that you are worshipping the sinless one.

Do you understand why it was important for Mary and Joseph to comply with the Law of Moses?

[Jesus said,] *"Do not think that I have come to abolish the Law or the Prophets; I have not come to abolish them but to fulfill them."*

MATTHEW 5:17

Dear Lord:

I look beyond the manger bed where Your infant body lay. I look to the man who lived a perfect life and died for my transgressions. I know it's fruitless for me to expect to live a life without sin. It simply isn't in me. But I know that Your sinless life covers me. It is in You that I am found righteous and given access to God the Father. I cannot keep the Law, but fortunately, You did—from the requirements at Your birth to the last breath You took on the cross. My confidence is not in myself. It is in You.

Amen.

"Great High Priest"

Since, then, we have a great high priest who has passed through the heavens, Jesus, the Son of God, let us hold fast to our confession. For we do not have a high priest who is unable to sympathize with our weaknesses, but we have one who in every respect has been tested as we are, yet without sin.

HEBREWS 4:14-15 NRSV

WHEN JESUS WAS BORN, there were two powerful forces oppressing God's people—the Romans and the religious establishment of the day, the priests. These priests were powerful and harsh, exacting from the people every letter of the law. They certainly had no compassion for those entrusted to their care. But when Jesus came, He became our *Great High Priest.* He lived among us so that He could understand our weaknesses and offer Himself as a perfect sacrifice for our sins. In His death, He did what priests are supposed to do—He atoned for our sins, not with the blood of animals, but with His own holy blood.

My Daddy Fixed Me

The company had gathered, all the children were playing outdoors, and Fran had just put the final trimmings on the Christmas feast. She was almost ready to reach for the dinner bell when a young boy with a frightened look on his face ran to the door and yelled, "Come quick! Steve got hurt."

Fran called to her husband, Jim, and together they ran out to the end of the paved driveway where their two-and-a-half-year-old son, Steve, had catapulted off a rolling plastic horse and landed on his chin. He had a gaping wound that would require stitches to heal.

The couple expressed regrets to their guests about the mealtime delay, picked up their crying child, jumped in the car, and headed for the hospital emergency room. When they arrived, restraining the tot was the worst part. With the child still howling, his medical doctor dad carefully applied local anesthetic to Steve's chin and sutured the cut. After the procedure was completed, Steve hopped off the table, took the red candy sucker offered by the nurse, and without a tear in his eyes, proudly announced, "My daddy fixed me!"

Just like this child who trusted his dad to fix him, we too can trust our heavenly Father to help us with all our needs. ✤

The Story of the Christ Child

[READING FROM LUKE 2:25-28 MSG]

In Jerusalem at the time, there was a man, Simeon by name, a good man, a man who lived in the prayerful expectancy of help for Israel. And the Holy Spirit was on him. The Holy Spirit had shown him that he would see the Messiah of God before he died. Led by the Spirit, he entered the Temple. As the parents of the child Jesus brought him in to carry out the rituals of the Law, Simeon took him into his arms and blessed God.

*F*or the nation of Israel, the appearance of the promised Messiah should have created a national celebration—but it did not. Most everyone was expecting someone quite different, a mighty warrior who would ride onto the scene and rid them of their barbaric rulers. Christ's arrival as a child did not register with them. But it was noticed and applauded by some—those humble few who had studied the Scriptures, who were watching daily, who knew that spiritual redemption must come before physical deliverance. Simeon was one of those. He recognized the child he held in his arms.

Sometimes, we too, want God to just deliver us from all our problems. In our difficulties, we fail to see God bringing about His purposes in our lives. But He promises to bring good out of every situation. We just need to see the big picture like Simeon did.

Are you in a difficult situation presently? Ask the Lord to help you see the eternal picture.

*And we know that all things work together
for good to them that love God, to them who
are the called according to his purpose.*
ROMANS 8:28 KJV

Dear Lord:

Open my eyes to look beyond my current circumstances and see Your eternal plans for me. Help me to
realize that You really do have my best interest at heart.
Thank You that You are using every event to conform me to
the image of Your Son, Jesus. Help me to look forward to the
day when I will see You face to face even though now I see
only a reflection (1 Cor. 13:12).

Amen.

"Messiah"

The first thing Andrew did was to find his brother
Simon and tell him, "We have found the Messiah" (that
is, the Christ). And he brought him to Jesus.
JOHN 1:41-42

THE JEWS WAITED FOR the coming of the *Messiah* with the same longing—the same fervor—that believers wait today for His second coming. It was their hope in a dark and dangerous world. When He did indeed appear, though, they did not see Him; their hearts obscured their vision. They were not looking for someone to restore them to God their Father. They were looking for someone to exact revenge on their enemies and place them in a position of power and authority. They did not recognize the infant in His humble surroundings. Only those whose eyes had been opened to see Him knew His worth. When He comes again, will He find us waiting with open hearts and eyes to see Him?

Oh, My Head!

Kristi's favorite part of Christmas was helping her mother unpack the manger scene. Around the first of November, Kristi and Mother cleared the top of the piano to make room for the hand-carved holy family, wise men, and townspeople figures which came with interesting stories about their search for the Savior.

Each figure was lovingly removed from its original box, marked with a detailed description.

"Hurry, Mom, hurry! Find my man," said Kristi.

Mother checked the remaining boxes and retrieved the one marked "man with headache."

"Here he is, Kristi. Find him a spot to see Jesus."

"Okay, Mom, tell me again. Why does he have a headache?" Kristi never tires of hearing the same story again.

Each year the figures seem to come alive as Kristi's mother tells made-up stories about the hardships endured on the way to the manger.

Over his arm, Man with Headache carries a small food basket. Clutching his hat, he holds his right hand to his stomach. He holds his head with his left hand. Perhaps he had worked hard in the few days before his journey. His wife and three small children are left behind. Along the way, the man has slept poorly, as this is his first lengthy journey away from his family. Because his children are young, Man with Headache had to find a willing friend to oversee his flock while he is gone. Despite the difficulties of the trip, the man's anticipation of seeing Jesus makes it all worthwhile.

This time of year is extremely busy. Don't let it overwhelm you, or you may find yourself with a headache! Let the anticipation of His coming make everything worthwhile. ❖

The Story of the Christ Child

[READING FROM LUKE 2:29-32 MSG]

"God, you can now release your servant;
release me in peace as you promised.
With my own eyes I've seen your salvation;
it's now out in the open for everyone to see:
A God-revealing light to the non-Jewish nations,
and of glory for your people Israel."

*I*magine the scene: Simeon standing before the altar, the child in his arms. As he looked down into the infant's face, he knew. God's promise had been fulfilled. He was holding God's answer to his prayers, the Messiah promised in the Scriptures. He was holding God's salvation—salvation for his nation, salvation for himself. He could die in peace now. He had seen the fulfillment of God's plan.

God had put into Simeon's heart the desire to see the Messiah before his time on earth was done. It was part of God's plan for his life. And Simeon saw it come to fruition—what a joy!

What has God put into your heart? Will you be faithful till you see it fulfilled?

Therefore, my dear brothers, stand firm. Let nothing move you. Always give yourselves fully to the work of the Lord, because you know that your labor in the Lord is not in vain.

1 CORINTHIANS 15:58

Dear Lord:

Thank You for the dreams and desires You've placed in my heart. Help me to be faithful like Simeon—always watching—and never giving up until I see the dreams You have for me come true.

Thank You for being faithful to the purpose that You came to accomplish and that You never gave up even though it cost You Your life. As a result, my sins have been wiped away and I have hope. Thank you—You are faithful!

Amen.

"Bright Morning Star"

"I, Jesus, have sent my angel to give you this testimony
for the churches. I am the Root and the Offspring of
David, and the bright Morning Star."
REVELATION 22:16

AS JESUS, MARY, AND JOSEPH huddled together that cold night in Bethlehem, a star shone overhead. We know little about that star—where it came from, how it led the shepherds and the Magi. We wonder why it did not draw the attention of others in the area. We don't have the answers, but we do know what that star represented. It was a guiding star, a celebratory star, a star designed to confirm the birth of God's own Son. The book of Revelation confirms the identity of the Christ by attributing to Him the name *Bright Morning Star.* He is indeed the light in the dark night of human failing. He is indeed the star that guides humankind to newness of life and fellowship with their Creator. He is the star that celebrates God's love for His children.

Live Nativity

    Ridgecrest Baptist Church in Greenville, Texas, holds an annual live nativity in their community. The pageant has become a local tradition and received recognition by *Texas Highways Magazine*. Charter members of the church sew elaborate costumes to depict the nativity characters. Each participant stands motionless for one-half hour before being replaced by the next shift of folks dressed in identical costumes.

    One year the nativity committee decided to take the scene to the Crossroads shopping mall across the street from the church. The shepherds entered from the north entrance, the wise men from the south, and the holy family—Mary, Joseph, and the infant Jesus—from the east. They converged in a central open area and assumed their positions.

Bonnie, the nativity director that year, said, "I was so surprised when a mother and her two children spontaneously approached the manger. Then what happened was so touching. There in the busy mall, the three of them knelt beside the wooden manger, and I could hear the mother praying. In a few minutes, they went on their way."

Later, another family came by and the children asked their mother, "What is that?" to which she coarsely replied, "I don't know."

Bonnie stepped forward and gently gave them an information sheet that described the significance of Christ's birth. That night they learned that Jesus came to give them eternal life, a gift their money could not buy. ❖

The Story of the Christ Child

[READING FROM LUKE 2:33-35 MSG]

*Jesus' father and mother were speechless with surprise
at these words. Simeon went on to bless them, and
said to Mary his mother,*

> *"This child marks both the failure and
>   the recovery of many in Israel,
> A figure misunderstood and contradicted—
>   the pain of a sword-thrust through you—
> But the rejection will force honesty,
>   as God reveals who they really are."*

$\mathscr{S}$imeon had read the Scriptures. He knew that this child would not have an easy life. He didn't have the details, how the eternal drama would play itself out, but he knew enough. The majority would fail to see the Messiah for who He was. He would be rejected and persecuted. And He would lay down His life for this same humanity that rejected Him.

Instead of pursuing His own desires, Jesus surrendered to God's plan for His life. The result was your salvation. Jesus paid the ultimate price—He gave up everything for you. Will you do the same for Him?

As you reflect upon all He has done for you during this Advent season, is there any part of your life that you need to give Him?

He [Jesus] answered, "What's written in God's Law? How do you interpret it?"

He [The religion scholar] said, "That you love the Lord your God with all your passion and prayer and muscle and intelligence—and that you love your neighbor as well as you do yourself."

LUKE 10:26–27 MSG

Dear Lord:

Thank You for giving Your all for me. Help me to be willing to give my all for You. That scares me somehow, but help me see that Your love always seeks my best so I do not need to be afraid. I worship You now on bended knee and with a heart submissive to Your will, ready to take up my assignment in the eternal drama.

Amen.

"Lion of Judah"

✦

Then one of the elders said to me,
"Do not weep! See, the Lion of the tribe of Judah,
the Root of David, has triumphed. He is able
to open the scroll and its seven seals."
REVELATION 5:5

THE MIGHTY WARRIOR EXPECTED to deliver Israel was not a misnomer. Though His mission here on earth was to exact spiritual deliverance and restore humankind to their Creator, He will one day deliver the world from the clutches of Satan. Ancient prophesy proclaims that such a leader will come from the priestly tribe of Judah. He will be the ultimate deliverer. Jesus is so many things to us. But we must not forget that one day He will exact God's vengeance on the earth. We will all see Him, leading the heavenly forces into battle. Like a lion, He will devour all evil in His path. The *Lion of the Tribe of Judah*, our Jesus, will prevail.

Following the Star

As Carol drove the two boys home from church, they chattered on and on about the lesson they had learned in Sunday school, but Carol couldn't concentrate on what they were saying. She had been struggling to find a job to help meet their family's financial needs. Yet every lead she followed turned out to be a dead end. However, as she waited at a stoplight, something made her listen more closely to the boys' excited chattering.

"These kings saw this star a long way off, and they came prepared with their gifts, and they followed it a long way before they ever got to the baby," six-year-old Rich said excitedly.

"They took their camels into the desert," three-year-old Robby declared.

"And those kings did all of that, but the Bible says they never got happy until they got to the place where Baby Jesus was," Rich continued. "They kept on going until they got to the baby. They followed the star and found joy. Isn't that great, Mom?"

"Yeah, they followed the star to joy," Robby echoed. "Isn't *that* great, Mom?"

Carol thought about the story of the kings. They might have felt that they were following a dead end when they traveled through miles of desert. But they kept going and kept trusting and eventually had something to be happy about.

As they turned into the driveway, Carol began to smile. Maybe her job search wasn't just a series of dead ends after all. Maybe she was really following a star to joy. "Come on, boys," she grinned. "Last one to the house is a king's camel!" �֎

The Story of the Christ Child

[READING FROM LUKE 2:36–40 MSG]

Anna the prophetess was also there, a daughter of
Phanuel from the tribe of Asher. She was by now a
very old woman. She had been married seven years
and a widow for eighty-four. She never left the Temple
area, worshiping night and day with her fastings and
prayers. At the very time Simeon was praying, she
showed up, broke into an anthem of praise to God,
and talked about the child to all who were waiting
expectantly for the freeing of Jerusalem.

When they finished everything required by God in
the Law, they returned to Galilee and their own town,
Nazareth. There the child grew strong in body and
wise in spirit. And the grace of God was on him.

*B*y this time, Mary must have had a heart full. So much had happened to her in such a short time. A year ago, she had been a carefree young girl, nothing out of the ordinary, just a pretty face in a crowd. But now, what wonders she had seen, what glory she had witnessed.

The angel had explained it, and Mary knew that nothing about the last year of her life had been natural. It had been supernatural—God-natural. All of it—the pregnancy, the birth, the unexpected worshippers, even the application of the Law—had been out of her hands. For now, her assignment was to be mother. But one day, she too would fall at His feet and worship Him. Her heart would break as she watched Him suffer—and shout in jubilation when she saw Him risen from the grave. Her Son, her Savior, her Lord.

Will you worship the Christ, rejoicing in anticipation of the supernatural events you will see as you give yourself fully to Him?

Ascribe to the LORD, O mighty ones,
ascribe to the LORD glory and strength.
Ascribe to the LORD the glory due his name;
worship the LORD in the splendor of his holiness.
PSALM 29:1-2

Dear Lord:

As I turn my heart to worship, continue Your sanctifying work in my life. Make known to me every aspect of the Christ as He reigns in my heart during this Christmas season and throughout the years to come. Make of me Your royal subject, with bowed head and bended knee honoring and praising You both for what You do and who You are. May I be pleasing in Your sight, offering my life as an act of worship as well. What a privilege it is to serve You. What an honor to be Your child. What a glorious expectation to be part of Your eternal plan.

Amen.

"The Word"

In the beginning was the Word, and the Word
was with God, and the Word was God.
He was with God in the beginning.
JOHN 1:1-2

THE BABY BORN IN A STABLE and placed in a crude manger was a new life—tiny hands and fingers, feet and toes. But inside, He was an old soul. He had, in fact, been around since the dawn of time—certainly even before that. The Bible says that He created it all—the earth and everything in it. John, inspired by the Holy Spirit, put it all into context when he proclaimed that God was keeping His promise to His people and to Himself by sending the Son, His companion from eternity past, in a real sense, Himself. In Jesus, God literally fulfilled His *Word*. May you understand that with your heart this Christmas season as you worship Him with all your heart, soul, mind, and strength.

For the Least of These

In Henry Van Dyke's classic work, *The Other Wise Man*, Artaban plans to join his three friends in Babylon as they follow the star in search of the King. He has three jewels to offer as gifts to the Christ Child.

But before he arrives, Artaban finds a feverish, poor Hebrew exile in the road. Torn between duty and desire, he ultimately stays and ministers for hours to the dying man. By the time Artaban arrives at the Bethlehem stable, the other Magi have left. A note encourages him to follow them through the desert.

But Artaban has given the dying man his last provisions, so he returns to the city, sells one of his three jewels, and buys camels and food. In the deserted town of Bethlehem, a frightened woman cradling her baby tells Artaban that Joseph, Mary, and the babe fled to Egypt to escape Herod's soldiers who are killing all the baby boys in the city. He offers a ruby to one of Herod's soldiers to save the woman's child.

Heartbroken that he has spent two of his gifts already, Artaban wanders for years seeking to worship the new King. He discovers no Baby King but finds many poor, sick, and hungry to feed, clothe, and comfort.

Many years later in Jerusalem, white-haired Artaban hears about a king being executed. He rushes toward Calvary to ransom the king with his last jewel. But instead, Artaban ends up rescuing a young woman from slavery.

At the end of the story, Artaban laments the turn of events. He wanted to bring gifts and minister to the King of kings. Yet he spent his fortune helping people in need. The Lord comforts him with these words: "Verily I say unto you, Inasmuch as ye have done it unto one of the least of these my brethren, ye have done it unto me" (Matthew 25:40 KJV).

The celebration of Christmas is more than just a holiday. And worship is more than mere words or gifts. Like the fourth wise man learned, real worship is a way of life. ❈

The Birth of Jesus Christ

[READING FROM MATTHEW 1:18—2:23 NCV]

**DAY
28**

*This is how the birth of Jesus Christ came about. His
mother Mary was engaged to marry Joseph, but before
they married, she learned she was pregnant by the
power of the Holy Spirit. Because Mary's husband,
Joseph, was a good man, he did not want to disgrace
her in public, so he planned to divorce her secretly.*

*While Joseph thought about these things, an angel of
the Lord came to him in a dream. The angel said, "Joseph,
descendant of David, don't be afraid to take Mary as
your wife, because the baby in her is from the Holy Spirit.
She will give birth to a son, and you will name him Jesus,
because he will save his people from their sins."*

*All this happened to bring about what the Lord
had said through the prophet: "The virgin will be pregnant. She will have a son, and they will name him
Immanuel," which means "God is with us."*

*When Joseph woke up, he did what the Lord's angel
had told him to do. Joseph took Mary as his wife, but
he did not have sexual relations with her until she
gave birth to the son. And Joseph named him Jesus.*

WISE MEN COME TO VISIT JESUS

*Jesus was born in the town of Bethlehem in Judea
during the time when Herod was king. When Jesus was
born, some wise men from the east came to Jerusalem.
They asked, "Where is the baby who was born to be
the king of the Jews? We saw his star in the east and
have come to worship him."*

*When King Herod heard this, he was troubled, as
well as all the people in Jerusalem. Herod called a*

meeting of all the leading priests and teachers of the law and asked them where the Christ would be born. They answered, "In the town of Bethlehem in Judea. The prophet wrote about this in the Scriptures:

'But you, Bethlehem, in the land of Judah,
    are important among the tribes of Judah.
A ruler will come from you
    who will be like a shepherd for my people Israel.'"

Micah 5:2

Then Herod had a secret meeting with the wise men and learned from them the exact time they first saw the star. He sent the wise men to Bethlehem, saying, "Look carefully for the child. When you find him, come tell me so I can worship him too."

After the wise men heard the king, they left. The star that they had seen in the east went before them until it stopped above the place where the child was. When the wise men saw the star, they were filled with joy. They came to the house where the child was and saw him with his mother, Mary, and they bowed down and worshiped him. They opened their gifts and gave him treasures of gold, frankincense, and myrrh. But God warned the wise men in a dream not to go back to Herod, so they returned to their own country by a different way.

JESUS' PARENTS TAKE HIM TO EGYPT

After they left, an angel of the Lord came to Joseph in a dream and said, "Get up! Take the child and his mother and escape to Egypt, because Herod is starting to look for the child so he can kill him. Stay in Egypt until I tell you to return."

So Joseph got up and left for Egypt during the night with the child and his mother. And Joseph stayed in Egypt until Herod died. This happened to bring about what the Lord had said through the prophet: "I called my son out of Egypt."

HEROD KILLS THE BABY BOYS

When Herod saw that the wise men had tricked him, he was furious. So he gave an order to kill all the baby boys in Bethlehem and in the surrounding area who were two years old or younger. This was in keeping with the time he learned from the wise men. So what God had said through the prophet Jeremiah came true:

> *"A voice was heard in Ramah*
> *of painful crying and deep sadness:*
> *Rachel crying for her children.*
> *She refused to be comforted,*
> *because her children are dead."*

Jeremiah 31:15

JOSEPH AND MARY RETURN

After Herod died, an angel of the Lord spoke to Joseph in a dream while he was in Egypt. The angel said, "Get up! Take the child and his mother and go to the land of Israel, because the people who were trying to kill the child are now dead."

So Joseph took the child and his mother and went to Israel. But he heard that Archelaus was now king in Judea since his father Herod had died. So Joseph was afraid to go there. After being warned in a dream, he went to the area of Galilee, to a town called Nazareth, and lived there. And so what God had said through the prophets came true: "He will be called a Nazarene."

1. Craig McDonald, *Greenville Herald Banner* (December 26, 1997).
2. Steven Ger, "The Undying Flame," *Kindred Spirit* (Winter, 1999).
3. *Dallas Morning News* (February 2, 1992).
4. Gerald Bath, "Long Walk Included," http://www.sermons.org/Christmasillustrations1-1999.html#4 (accessed June 11, 2007).